FROM A MIDDLE-AGED DAD
TO A TEENAGE DAUGHTER

FROM A MIDDLE-AGED DAD TO A TEENAGE DAUGHTER

by

Grant Sandercock-Brown

Illustrations by
Berni Georges

Salvation Books
The Salvation Army International Headquarters
London, United Kingdom

First published 2008

Copyright © 2008
The General of The Salvation Army

ISBN 978-0-85412-767-2

Cover design by Berni Georges

SALVATION BOOKS

Published by Salvation Books
The Salvation Army International Headquarters
101 Queen Victoria Street, London EC4V 4EH
United Kingdom

Printed by UK Territory Print & Design Unit

CONTENTS

FOREWORD

From A Middle Aged Dad To A Teenage Daughter – aimed at the teenage market, but of interest and value to parents – is based on genuine letters written by an Australian corps officer, Captain Grant Sandercock-Brown, to his own daughter ... hence the title. The author is well known to readers of *The Officer* as one of that magazine's regular columnists. His original letters aimed to explain aspects of Christian belief in the contemporary language and style of young people, and this book sets out to do the same. It is wittily illustrated by Berni Georges, a designer on the staff at International Headquarters. Topics covered include sin, Hell, the death of a child, science-versus-religion, holiness, sex, the Trinity, the Church, the gospel and prayer. They're weighty subjects, but dealt with here with a light – yet authoritative – touch that will be appreciated by readers of all ages.

Charles King, Major
Literary Secretary
International Headquarters
London, February 2008

INTRODUCTION

To Isabel,

I've been writing to you for a while now about some really important things about you and God. I've decided to put them all together for you in case you want to think about them some more.

Dad

Decision time

One

Darling,

Sorry we haven't been able to sit down and talk but what with chatting online, texting, phone calls, homework, sport and music lessons (and the stuff *you* do as well) we don't often have a chance, so I'll set my thoughts down and you can read them at your leisure.

I wanted to talk to you about decision-making. When I was a boy, life seemed a bit simpler (there wasn't even one McDonald's in Australia) so here's some stuff about making good decisions that might relieve your stress.

I know you want to make decisions that please your Mum and Dad, and please God, and you've got some big ones coming up. Elective subjects at school, balancing your budget, whether to save for the VW or the Mini, your career after school, Dave or Chris. How does all that fit in with God's plan for your life, and what is God's plan anyway?

Well relax, I know God's plan for your life. He wants you to be like Jesus. That's it! Often when we read the words 'God's will' in the Bible we think of 'God's plan' as in God's roadmap of decisions. But that's not quite what it means. The word 'plan' in the original Bible language means 'wish' or 'desire'. God's will is not a blueprint for your life but his desire for your life, and his desire is that you be holy (which really means trying, with God's help, to be like Jesus).

I suspect God doesn't care whether you choose the Beetle or the Mini but he does care about how you drive it. So don't worry about deciding between studying Italian or Japanese, or between a Nokia or a Motorola, netball or hockey.

God's concern is not what subject you choose but what sort of a student you are. He doesn't care about brand names but how you spend your money. He doesn't mind which sport you play but he's vitally concerned with how you play it. So choose the subjects you like and which suit your gifts. Choose the car you can afford and be a patient, responsible driver. Choose teaching or medicine, whichever door opens. Either the University of Technology or Sydney University is fine. Choose friends, and particularly boyfriends, who will encourage and help you when you ask the question, 'What would Jesus do?'

Don't worry that by making a particular decision you might be falling away from God's plan for your life. His desire is that you be like Jesus. That will always be what matters most, not which subjects or course or career.

So don't stress about all those big decisions coming up, don't feel that you don't know God's will – you do! Be like Jesus.

By the way I do have a favourite out of Dave and Chris and I'll be happy to let you know which one!

With my love,

Dad

PS Tidying your room could be part of God's plan. Waddya think?

Losing your temper isn't the right thing to do
but it won't keep you out of Heaven

Two

Darling,

I want to talk about another subject that might help you in these amazing and challenging teenage years. I remember when I was a teenager (back in the 70s when ABBA was big - I can see you rolling your eyes but stay with me) I was often worried that when I did the wrong thing I was in trouble not only with my parents but with God as well. I wasn't sure where I stood with God. Did my sinning mean I was in danger of Hell? I felt pretty insecure about this whole Christianity thing.

Well, I want to reassure you that doing the wrong thing doesn't mean God stops loving you. Nor does it mean you've been 'red-carded' out of the Kingdom of Heaven. God loves you and me as sinners, and he sent to Jesus to die for us, not in spite of our sin but because of it. That's pretty amazing.

The fact is, we're all sinners, whether we've just sinned or not. I'm afraid that not sinning for a week won't make you a saint. But that's OK because that's true for all of us. It's what God does that makes us saints. The Bible talks about the fact that when we become followers of Jesus we're not regulated by rules but given grace. That means God freely forgives you and you're a saint, not because you deserve it but because God loves you. That's awesome!

What it means is that, as long as you keep making decisions towards Christ and want to be his follower, he won't let you fall. Losing your temper at your little sister isn't the right thing to do (although you'd be amazed at how annoying your Aunty was back in the 70s) but it won't keep you out of Heaven.

Committing a sin doesn't mean you're no longer a Christian. Christians sin too. You're not regulated by rules but given grace. That's not to say if you keep choosing to get angry at your sister you won't find yourself facing away from Jesus and on a journey in another direction (choosing sin as opposed to trying to choose the good). But be reassured that while God is not happy with sin, he loves you, and your trust in him means that your loving God is holding you, his saint, in the palm of his hand.

You are his child. Be assured of that. God's heart might ache when you do the wrong thing but his love for you is unchanged. God is your loving Father and his love is secure, and don't you forget it!

With my love

Dad

PS Tidying your room is not a sin!

Little kids don't know right from wrong

Three

Darling,

I know you've been upset by the thought of little babies dying. It seems so unfair. I can't explain why God allows things like that to happen. Sometimes I just have to trust him even when I can't for the life of me understand what he's doing. I guess that's what real trust is. However let me reassure you about one thing. Little children who die go to Heaven to be with Jesus.

You know that my little brother (who would have been your uncle and 35 today) died when he was small. Well, as a teenager I always believed he was in Heaven. But was it just wishful thinking? Was he really with God? I've studied this subject a lot and let me say that I'm really sure that little children who die go to Heaven.

A long time ago one of the earliest Christian teachers, called Augustine, said that everybody was born guilty of sin, even little babies! And because they were guilty, if they died they didn't go to Heaven. Many people since have followed his lead, basing their view on an obscure text that, in one translation, says 'all people sinned in Adam' and are therefore born guilty of sin.

But the Bible tells us that little kids don't know right from wrong. They can't be guilty until they really know they're doing the wrong thing.

You can see what a heartache it would be if a mum or dad thought their baby was born guilty. It's why some of your friend's churches have placed so much importance on being baptised, or being part of a Christian family – they believe that will fix the guilt thing.

They needn't worry. When you were born, you weren't guilty of sin (you did look a bit like E.T., but I'm sure that's not a sin). You belonged to God. As you grew up, God expected more from you. God's expectations are unique to each person and it's true that one day you will be accountable before him. But you can trust him to be fair.

One day, with his disciples, Jesus picked up some little children, gave them a cuddle and said, 'The Kingdom of Heaven belongs to such as these.'

I'm sure the parents felt a whole lot better when they heard that. Little children belong to God. Sure, they don't have 'faith' in Jesus like older people, but you couldn't really expect them to! As Angelica from *Rugrats* would say: 'They're only babies.' It appears that little children belong to the Kingdom because God is really loving.

So don't worry, God is looking after the babies.

With my love,

Dad

PS Thanks for tidying your room on Saturday. It's amazing how by Monday it looked as if you hadn't!

Science has never proved that miracles can't happen

Four

Darling,

Since it's a Saturday, and you're sleeping in, I just want to share some thoughts on the stuff you're studying in science at the moment. I know it can be a bit threatening if people say science proves God doesn't exist, or science proves the Bible wrong. Sometimes it feels like you have to choose between being a Christian and believing in science. I don't think that's true. Let me explain why.

In the 1860s a man called Charles Darwin came up with the theory of evolution, and one of the things he said was that humans developed from apes. This pretty much shocked most Christians and lots of them weren't sure what to do. This was after a period called the enlightenment (a bit like in cartoons where the light bulb goes on over people's heads), when famous thinkers said that eventually humans would be able to explain everything.

So, lots of people were saying they didn't believe in God or all that stuff in the Bible about miracles. In fact even some Christians said they didn't believe in miracles any more, not even Jesus rising from the dead!

A century later another theory was put forward, saying a 'big bang' started the whole universe. This challenged Christians even more (this was when I was at school, at a time when when TV was black-and-white, computers were as big as your bedroom and pocket money was just a few coins a week).

Well, what to do? Say that science is right and the Bible wrong? Or that scientists are wrong and the Bible is right? Or do you say it doesn't matter, you can still be a Christian anyway?

I think you can take a bit from all three views.

Firstly, science is right. By that I mean the things scientists say that are science. It seems our world is much older than the 6,000 years of human history recorded in the Bible, for example. But, at the same time, science has never proved that miracles can't happen. Science works by explaining things it can examine and prove in experiments. Science can't possibly prove that Jesus didn't rise from the dead.

As for Christians who don't believe in miracles, it doesn't matter how smart you are, if you think the miracles in the Bible aren't miracles, that's an idea you bring to the Bible, not one you get from it. The Bible pretty much expects God to do miracles from beginning to end.

And people who think science can prove the Bible isn't history need to think again. History is the written and spoken stories from our past, and science isn't even the same subject! It would be like your science teacher saying your English teacher is wrong about a poem's meaning because he or she has analysed the paper it was written on. Science isn't about meanings.

An interesting thing is that scientists proved the big bang theory by maths and physics, using rules that you know. Things like pi = 3.142857. But hang on! Why is pi always pi? Who made up the rules of maths?

Secondly, you can say that the Bible is right. It's absolutely true about its subject – God. Sometimes people try and turn the Bible into a science book and try to prove science wrong. But that's pretty hard to do. The people who wrote the Bible weren't scientists and weren't trying to write science. When they are talking about things like creation they are talking about something God told them, because obviously they weren't there! The Bible is a book about God. What the Bible does say all the way through is that God created the world (not how he did it); that God created humans (again, not how he did it) and that God loves us as the best bit of his creation. You can believe that with all your heart!

Thirdly, you can say that 'science vs the Bible' is not the most important thing. We can be pretty sure that science has a lot to learn and that theories like evolution and the big bang are still works in progress – but also that our understanding of God is a work in progress.

What matters most is not science but another subject completely, the Jesus subject (and all serious students of this subject get a prize). Jesus lived and

15

died and rose from the dead and he loves you infinitely more than even I do. And one day you'll be in Heaven and you can personally ask him all the 'why' questions you want, although I have a sneaking suspicion that they just won't seem to matter anymore.

With my love,

Dad

PS Some scientists might look at the chaos of your room and wonder if life can exist in such a hostile environment!

Being a Christian will sometimes be tough

Five

Darling,

I just wanted to let you know that you are a holy person. No, it doesn't mean you're perfect but it does mean that God has made you holy. Did you know you were holy? That's pretty amazing but it's true. And, in fact, in our brand of being a Christian we don't just mean God sees you as holy but that he makes you holy inside.

What does 'being holy inside' mean, I hear you ask? It means that when you're a follower of Jesus he purifies your heart so that you are a new you. It doesn't mean you are flawless or sinless or not yourself any more, or that you will be an angel. But it does mean you can completely love God and completely love other people just like he wants you to.

You see, when you get saved you become God's person, a follower of Jesus, and you are his and holy. But he also wants you to grow more and more like him in your lifelong journey with him.

Some Christians believe that's all there is to it. They think being a Christian is then a question of trying to be good, but with sin still in your heart. But I believe there is something more, that God hasn't stopped doing miracles in our lives and that he can change us inside; that we take a giant leap forward on our journey to be like Jesus. He purifies our heart.

For some people this happens when they first become Christians, for some people it happens later on the journey. Basically it means I believe something awesome can happen inside people. God can change your heart and make you a radically different person in a nanosecond!

How does this happen? Some people think it's by having more of God, but it actually means God having more of you. They think its something supernatural added on, but it's really about who you already are being changed.

It's about offering Jesus your heart and mind, and praying: 'Give me a heart and mind like yours, Jesus.' From when I was your age (and flared jeans were popular for the first time) I've always been amazed at people telling their stories about how they knelt and prayed and asked God to change them and he did. Then they would stand up and you could see the change in them. It always astounds me and it always will.

Being a Christian will sometimes be tough. Being a follower of Jesus can be costly. But it's never depressing, because it also means you're a new person with Jesus in your new heart. It's like those television garden makeover shows. God comes into the garden of your heart and does a renovation job like you wouldn't believe. You're not left to struggle along by yourself with good advice on gardening. But you have to do all the work yourself. Nor is it about looking for a new garden in a different house. You will still be you.

It's about God radically changing the old garden, giving you a heart like Jesus. And that means you are perfectly capable of loving God and perfectly capable of loving others. Completely God's in your relationship with him and people!

Holy you!

With my love,

Dad

PS A makeover-type cleaning of your room could be a miracle (and would please your earthly father).

Boys and girls view sex differently

Six

Darling

I want to talk to you about an issue that is perhaps a bigger challenge for you than it was for me. It's sex. The challenge comes from a big change back in the 1960s (the sexual revolution) when people started to talk about sex much more openly. Since then it has become a common topic for television sitcoms, books, movies and in teen magazines.

It was said by many 'experts' that being open about sex would fix things and make society a better place. In some ways that's been true. Some of the unfairness and hypocrisy in sexual standards for men and women have been addressed. But in other ways I'm not so sure.

You see, when I was a kid, sex was seen, more or less, as something that was supposed to happen only between married people. But many kids today see sex as normal and healthy for everyone – not much different in that respect from going for a jog. Much of society regards it as ok for pretty well any consenting people to have sex.

I don't agree. Sex is not just like going for a jog. I've spoken to quite a few people about sex and every one of them can remember the first time they had sex. Virtually none of them can remember the first time they went for a jog!

I suspect we know in our hearts that sex should mean something more than just a bit of physical exercise. You can say sex is just exercise, and you can act as if it's just exercise, but you'll pay a price for doing so.

As a former teenager I also have to be honest and say that boys and girls view sex differently. In my experience, if a reasonably attractive girl walked up to a 16-year-old boy she hardly knew and said, 'I'd like to sleep with you', a lot of boys would jump at the chance. But if a reasonably attractive boy walked up to a girl he hardly knew and said, 'I'd like to sleep with you', few girls would.

From my experience, most teenage boys want to have sex. Most teenage girls are interested in sex but want it to mean something. Boys say, 'If it feels good do it.' Girls (wisely) want something more meaningful. Yes, it's true: girls are more mature than boys.

'If it feels good do it' is an impractical rule to live by. If we did, most of us would be unhealthy, lazy and have committed an untold number of petty crimes and traffic offences. 'If you feel like you want to have sex you should' is a silly statement and so is anyone who thinks it's true. It doesn't apply in any other area of our lives, so why would we think it does here? I'm telling you, if you feel like gorging yourself on food, don't. If you feel like slapping that silly person's face, don't. If you feel like exploring sex,

24

don't. Even if sex was just like any other appetite I would still say don't 'just do it'.

But it's not just another appetite. Your sexuality is the marvellous gift of a Creator God. It can one day be the sign and seal of your bond with your future husband. For that reason alone, it is worth being faithful to him. In the oldest part of the Bible it says that when people get married 'two become one', and that's a mystery to be explored with you and the very fortunate boy you'll marry (after a stern but fair test I have organised that involves a few simple questions, a lie detector test and DNA sample). Trust me, if you and he can say to each other, 'I've never made love to anyone else but you, and never will' it will be a wonderful moment that honours God's desire for your life.

Being a teenager can be tough in the 21st century. Not sleeping with anyone until you are married is challenging, because society is loudly telling you something different. You have been, and will be, bombarded with pressures from the world around you that I never had to face. But don't despair, all of you – your mind, your heart and your desires – is a gift from God. Use it as he would wish. He will help you.

With my love,

Dad

PS I would feel good if you tidied your room. So do it!

25

It would be like a baby explaining adolescence

Seven

Darling,

I just thought I'd try and explain something unique about believing in Jesus. It's how he is connected to God and to the Holy Spirit. For me this is probably one of the hardest things to understand in being a Christian.

What Christians finally worked out about the connection of Jesus, God and the Spirit (the Holy Trinity) wasn't decided on until centuries after Jesus lived on earth. You might say, 'It can't be important if lots of the early Christians didn't know it', and in one way that's true. Being a Christian is not about being able to explain and remember all the things Christians believe. But just because humans took a long time to work out that the world wasn't flat doesn't mean it's less true, or that we should still worry about falling off the edge. Once we know something to be true we need to try and understand what it means for us. And the exploration of God and what he is like is a fantastic thing worth doing just because we can.

While the Trinity thing wasn't all worked out straightaway, the Bible shows us that Jesus' followers experienced the 'three-in-one' bit. The first

Christians were Jews and they believed absolutely that there was one God. They also believed that the Jesus they had seen was Lord, and they could also feel the Spirit of God in their hearts. It took Christians a long time to explain the three-in-one thing but they experienced it right from the start. The teaching was an attempt to make clear the way they had encountered God.

When I was younger than you (and using a hair product called Brylcreem) adults tried to describe the Trinity using eggs or rainbows or water. None of these descriptions was particularly helpful for me. There's a good reason for that. The created can't explain the Creator.

God is so radically different to us that we can never fully describe him. It would be like a two-year-old being able to explain adolescence, the need for homework and why teenagers need mobile phones. Toddlers may live surrounded by these things but they could never explain them (few of us can). It's why, in the Bible, a guy called Paul said we only see a dim reflection of what things really are. There are some really important things in life that just can't be put in words.

When you (my beautiful daughter) was born, I physically saw a miracle. I felt its impact inside me and knew there was a miracle Designer who made it possible (apparently I held you and, for 40 minutes, cried and didn't say one thing that made sense). In Jesus I see God, I feel his Spirit in me and I know that there is a Creator God who wants me to know him. That's the Trinity.

If I could explain God, he wouldn't be God. The finite can't contain the infinite. It's OK if you can't work it all out.

Do you know what a paradox is? It's something that seems to be absurd or contradictory but is in fact true. In the end I accept the Trinity as an awesome paradox that I see, feel and know to be true but can't describe. God, his Spirit and Jesus are all connected. They are essentially one but undeniably three. You and I might never explain it but we can experience it, and that's what really matters.

With my love,

Dad

PS I also can't explain why the floor in your room keeps disappearing. Do you know what cupboards are for?

The Church isn't a building ... it's people

Eight

Darling,

I want to explain something about this sometimes strange tribe called Christians that we belong to, and the way we hang out with each other. Of course I'm talking here about the Church and all the different churches.

Church is an unusual word. There are quite a few religious words – like 'spirituality', 'temple' and 'sacred' – that lots of different religions use, Buddhists and Hindus for example. But Church pretty much belongs to Christians.

The sad thing is that quite a few people today are rather suspicious of the Church and Church leaders. That's a tragedy because it's our own doing. If nobody else uses the word, it's we Christians who give it its meaning. We have let God down rather badly in this respect.

So what is the Church, I hear you ask?

Well we use 'church' (with a small 'c') in quite a few ways: to describe a building, or an organisation, or the group of Christians we meet up with on a regular basis. However, it's probably the third of these that is most accurate. The Church (with a capital 'C') isn't a building, although it usually meets in one. The Church isn't an organisation with departments, although these things can be really helpful in supporting a group of churches.

In the first Christian century, people who wrote about the Church, like the apostle Paul, used the word mostly to mean a local gathering of people: a fellowship of believers who worshipped together. And we can be pretty sure that at first these local gatherings mainly met in people's homes. There's no archaeological evidence of big churches (as in buildings) during the first few hundred years after Jesus' death and resurrection. So Paul, and disciples like John, wrote letters to these house churches and addressed their letters to 'the Church in Corinth' or 'the Church in Ephesus'.

There's another meaning for the word 'Church' which is used less often but is spectacularly important. When Paul wrote to the Church in Ephesus he talked about all the believers in the world being part of 'one Body' of Christ. This is what is often called the catholic church (when catholic is spelt with a small 'c' it means universal). The Church (with a capital C) is a mystical spiritual connection between all the followers of Jesus.

So how do you become a member of the Church or of a church? Well it's quite simple. You believe and you belong. Do you believe in Jesus, and have you asked him to be in charge of your life? If so, you're already in the 'big C' Church. Do you belong to a group of Christians? Do you meet up with them for prayer and worship? You're also in a 'little c' church. It's really that simple.

Of course lots of different churches means lots of different ceremonies to recognise the fact that you believe and belong, but those are public, formal ways of acknowledging what has already taken place.

Of course, a church doesn't exist just for our benefit. We are the Body of Christ in the world, the real feet and hands of a spiritual Body. This means we need to do the work of Jesus in the world. But that's another story.

So if you believe in Jesus you're in. And, for all its faults, the Church is an amazing thing to be a part of, and I would say it's all the better for you being there!

With my love,

Dad

PS Feel free to use the hands and feet of your body to do a work of tidying in your room. It could also be a spiritual experience.

Jesus says, 'Come and let me share your pain'

Nine

Darling,

I want to write to you about the gospel. It's a word I'm sure you've heard before. For Christians it means the 'good news' about Jesus. In fact it actually means Jesus. Let me explain.

One day Jesus went into a synagogue, read a famous passage from an ancient prophecy and said, 'Today this is fulfilled in me.' And the next few years were even more amazing. Jesus went around saying things like, 'If anybody is really struggling with life and comes to me I will make it better, because I'm really humble.' Work that one out!

When talking to people, Jesus sometimes said, 'Your sins are forgiven.' That was a bit unusual because they actually hadn't done anything to him (it'd be like your sister hitting your brother and you saying to your sister, 'I forgive you.'). It doesn't make sense – unless somehow Jesus was the one sinned against, of course.

Jesus said unexpected things like that all the time. Not only that, he seemed to feel people's pain and know their hearts. He told people that anyone who had seen him had seen God, and, what's more he, Jesus, could help them. He repeatedly said that because of him, God's Kingdom had arrived and was beginning to grow.

And what a Kingdom! It wasn't a geographical kingdom with borders but a real connection with Jesus as Lord. It was God's radical reign beginning to take place in our world. It was a coming Kingdom where the blind can see, the poor are blessed, pain is healed and the last become the first.

When I was your age, kids in Sunday school were supposed to know Bible verses off by heart. All the smart-alecs (like me) would say the shortest one: 'Jesus wept.' I didn't realise it then, but it's actually a really important verse.

You see, one of Jesus' friends had died and the friend's sisters had pleaded for Jesus to come and do something. He came, but two days too late. Jesus knew it would be all right, he was going to raise his friend from the dead. But on the way to the tomb one of the sisters came to him and she was grief-stricken and crying – and Jesus wept. For no other reason than she was his friend and she was hurting.

Our world is hurting. There is so much pain and sadness and, well, sin really. Jesus says, 'Come and let me share your pain. Give it to me and I will take it and I will offer you healing and forgiveness and love. I will start the healing now. And one day when the Kingdom fully comes there will be no more crying and all tears will be wiped away.'

And that's the amazing good news: Jesus. The astonishing Jesus who lived an extraordinary life, died an extraordinary death and extraordinarily rose from the dead. In him we can see God and know how much God loves us.

To accept this good news is to be his. To be a Christian is to believe this gospel, to trust that Jesus is the answer. You see, I don't know all the answers, even though I sometimes act as if I do. I don't even know all the questions. But I know the one who is the answer, and that's good news.

With my love,

Dad

PS I had some other good news the other day: I saw some floor space in your room. I knew there was a carpet under those clothes.

God is not merely a distant observer

Ten

Darling,

Since you were born I've prayed for you. And all your life it's pretty much been the same prayer. I have asked God to look after you, to help you and to make himself known to you. You might ask, 'Why do I keep on praying the same prayer?' Surely if God answers prayer, one good prayer when you were a baby should have been sufficient?

It's an interesting question.

All I can say is that it's been really important for me to pray. Mainly because God wants me to. Jesus prayed all the time and explained to his friends and followers what prayer should be like, and he insisted that God as a loving Father would answer our prayers. So I take Jesus at his word.

I also pray because prayer changes me. Talking to God about the stuff of everyday life helps me put things into perspective. I'm much less self-opinionated when talking to him! Whenever I pray I remember Jesus and how much God loves me, and I am so grateful for what he has done in my life that the selfish thoughts and feelings that do him no honour fall away. I can feel the good that prayer does me.

But I also pray believing that God will answer my prayers. I don't say that because all my prayer requests have been answered with a 'yes'. In fact sometimes I have felt hurt by his 'no', because I truly believed he could do what I asked but he chose not to.

But here's the thing: I really disliked it when I was little and your Grandma demanded obedience merely by saying, 'Because I say so'. I always thought I'd never say that myself. But I have said it (as you know). However there were some things I couldn't explain to you when you were three. Not because I didn't want to but because you just couldn't understand, I needed you to trust me. It appears that my Heavenly Father requires the same of me.

So I still pray, believing my prayers matter to him. And it's not because of anything I do. God is not more likely to say 'yes' to my prayers because I pray a particular way. I don't think prayer works like that. God answers my prayers because he loves me, not because I am a good pray-er or have been especially clear in my request or because I believed really hard.

On the other hand, you may think that because God knows the future he's already decided what will happen, so your prayers don't change anything. If God already has everything worked out, do your prayers matter?

Yes they do. God is not some clockmaker who wound up the clock of history and is now letting it run its course. God is not merely a distant observer who has organised our whole life.

It's true that God is outside time and can see our future as well as our past. But God also sustains and governs all things. He keeps the world going now. Our world is a dynamic work in progress and God writes our prayers into history as we speak them. He is not the remote and distant God who occasionally intervenes with a miracle in response to a really good prayer. God hears your prayers and weaves his 'yes' and 'no' into your present and your future, working all things together for your good. We can be sure of this just as we can be sure of his absolute love for us.

So pray. Believe that, no matter how simple or faltering your prayers are, a loving Father God hears and answers you.

With my love,

Dad

PS You must tidy your room. Because I say so!

Prepared to face lions

Eleven

Darling,

I've been a Christian for a few years now and I really want you to be a Christian too. Not just so you can be like me (thankfully you look more like your Mum and are completely over the E.T. thing) but because being a follower of Jesus is the best thing that anybody can do. So I want to explain to you why I believe in him.

It's not so much because I believe in the authority of the Bible, although I do. The Bible is absolutely trustworthy as the greatest book ever written. But that's because it tells us about the world's greatest story, not because my English version is perfect.

I read the Bible because it reveals the Jesus I love. I don't love Jesus just because he's revealed in the Bible. The Jesus thing always comes first. What's really compelling for me is that that whole of the Christian story makes sense. And part of that story is what has happened in history since Jesus.

In the first few centuries after Jesus lived, the story of his life, death and resurrection was so powerful that, despite persecution, it infiltrated the whole of the Roman Empire. By the fourth century it had reached the court of the emperor himself. That's pretty impressive for the Jesus people who on the day Jesus was crucified consisted of a small group of brave but distraught women and scared and hiding men. Within a few years these same women and men would look Roman soldiers in the face and die saying, 'Jesus is Lord'.

The fact that people are willing to die for their belief in Jesus has always amazed and challenged me. And it appears that people were prepared to do so almost immediately after Jesus' time on earth. That's why I can't accept that Christianity is a made-up story or a legend that grew around a pretty average bloke. I wouldn't be prepared to face lions just because I really liked the stories and views of a builder I'd known for a couple of years!

Jesus' world was full of gullible people but it was also full of intelligent critics as well. Christians dying for a silly story would have forced the 'true story' out in the open. But there was no alternative 'true story'. Peter, Jesus' best friend, died because he knew Jesus was the Son of God, not because he knew he wasn't. By non-Christian standards, Peter had nothing to gain and everything to lose by his refusal to deny his Lord.

One of the extraordinary things that has happened in the past century or so is people writing books (like *The Da Vinci Code*) that talk about Jesus as a legend (not history), invented for some unexplained reason by the early Church.

Your uncle had a similar idea when he was your age. He was sure the whole 'Christian' thing had been made up by some adults to stop him having fun!

It seems to me that the 'Jesus as a legend' and your uncle's theory are running neck-and-neck in the believability stakes. To think that after 2,000 years you can discover what the story of Jesus was really about and that everybody else has been fooled until now is pretty astounding. To do so, you must assume you're smarter than everyone else (which seems rather impolite) or that there has been a huge secret conspiracy by the Church (your uncle's theory).

Neither can possibly be true. The institution of the Church has a pretty embarrassing record when it comes to keeping secrets! And I refuse to believe that hundreds of people were willing to die for a story they knew was a lie.

Without writing a book, winning an election or even winning a war, Jesus, the Son of God, changed the world. I absolutely believe that. You can too.

With my love,

Dad

PS I notice your bedroom door no longer fully opens. Is using a pile of clothes, books, shoes, CDs, belts and bags as a doorstop a deliberate plan on your part?

You are God's child, loved with an unfailing love

Twelve

Darling,

I just want to say one final thing, and that's about who you are, about your true identity (don't panic, I'm your real Dad ... look at your eyes). By that I mean your sense of self. Someone once said that to have a sense of identity is to know that you exist in the minds of others.

There's a great deal of truth in that. Lots of people who feel alone and faceless in the world often feel there is no-one who thinks about them or cares about them. We long to feel known by others, to feel we are in their minds and hearts. To actually feel that no-one knows you or notices you (not even to dislike you) would be awful.

Of course, you've existed in your Mum's and my eyes since before you were born. You are a child of many prayers, hopes and dreams. You exist in other's minds as a daughter, sister and a friend. You've been the object of much love in your life. When you were little I promised myself that I would do all I could to make sure you felt loved, and I've tried my best to make that happen. But there's something more than that.

You see, you exist in the mind of God. You are his child. Imagine how much I love you and multiply that a thousand times and you still won't have arrived at how God feels about his children. He knows the deepest thoughts of your heart.

A very famous poet in the Bible talked about this. He said to God: 'You are acquainted with all my ways. There is not a word on my tongue that you don't know. You have laid your hand on me. If I take the wings of the morning and dwell in the uttermost parts of the sea, behold you are there.'

That's a really reassuring idea from our Father God. It's a beautiful thought which humbles me and comforts me at the same time.

Above all things, in the deepest part of your being, know this: the greatest truth about you is not that you are my child but that you are God's child, loved with an unfailing love. It may be that one day, whether by your choice or not, you 'take the wings of the morning' and feel that your sense of self is being lost. One day you may feel confused and wounded and alone, doubting your existence in the mind of others. If that happens, remember that God is still there. Remember that you matter to God. He cares for you, and you have never left the palm of his hand.

With my love,

Dad

PS I walk past your bedroom every night and actually don't think about whether it's messy or not. Rather, I feel comforted that you are there. You are a precious gift to me, and only God loves you more than I do.